All

AMERICA

Facts & Fun

Fran Newman-D'Amico

DOVER PUBLICATIONS, INC.
Mineola, New York

Bibliographical Note

All About America: Facts & Fun is a new work, first published by
Dover Publications, Inc., in 2008.

International Standard Book Number

ISBN-13: 978-0-486-46573-9
ISBN-10: 0-486-46573-X

Manufactured in the United States by Courier Corporation
46573X04
www.doverpublications

Note

In this fun-filled little book, you will learn "all about America"! From the "Red, White, and Blue" flag to the official flower, you will find lots and lots of interesting facts about the U.S. as you enjoy the puzzles and coloring pages. You'll help a Pony Express rider find the way through a maze, connect the dots to see a picture of the plane flown by the Wright Brothers, and even count the rings on California redwood trees to find their age. There is a Solutions section, beginning on page 53, in case you need to check your answers.

Get your pencil ready, and make sure you have some crayons, so that you can enjoy coloring in the pages after you have finished the puzzles. Enjoy!

Here's the "Red, White, and Blue"—the American flag. Color 7 stripes red, starting with the top stripe and coloring every other stripe. Then color the area behind the stars blue.

4

I = ✏️ L = ❀ F = ◯ O = ✳️

R = ✖️ C = ▢ A = ✌️ N = ✳

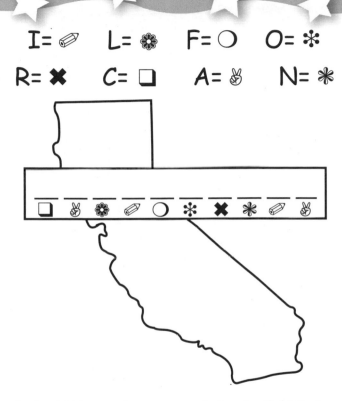

In the 1840s, people went west during the Gold Rush to get rich. Use the code at the top to spell the name of the state where many people searched for gold.

HET   =_ _ _

EITWH =_ _ _ _ _

OSHUE =_ _ _ _ _

This is America's most-visited historic home. It has 132 rooms, 412 doors, and 147 windows! Unscramble the words to write this famous building's name.

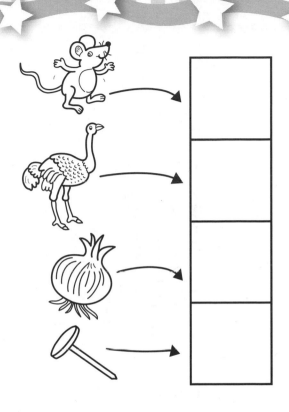

On July 20, 1969, Neil Armstrong became the first person to walk here. Write the first letter of each picture in the box to find the answer.

The Statue of Liberty was a gift from France for the one hundredth birthday of America's independence. It is a symbol of freedom.

Now look closely at the picture. Five things have changed! Find and circle them all.

The Pony Express used 200 riders to carry mail between Missouri and California in the early 1840s. Help this Pony Express rider find his way to deliver the mail.

AMERICAN

_____   _____

_____   _____

_____   _____

_____   _____

_____   _____

_____   _____

_____   _____

How many words can you make using the letters in the word AMERICAN? If you need more room, use a separate sheet of paper.

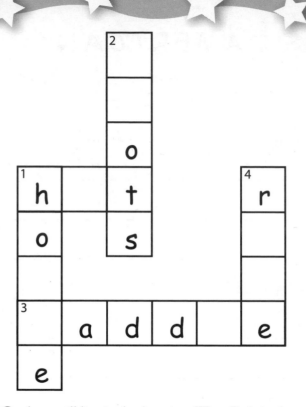

Cowboys still live in the American West. Did you know that they sometimes sang songs to their cattle at night?

1 down

4 down

1 across

2 down

3 across

Use the pictures above to solve the puzzle on the opposite page. The number next to each picture tells you where the word belongs in the puzzle.

▲ = N   ● = G   ◇ = B   ⊚ = L

☽ = I   ◩ = C   ♉ = A   ☆ = O

⊚ ☆ ●

◩ ♉ ◇ ☽ ▲

Abraham Lincoln, the sixteenth president, was born on February 12, 1809, in Kentucky. Use the code to find out what kind of house Lincoln was born in.

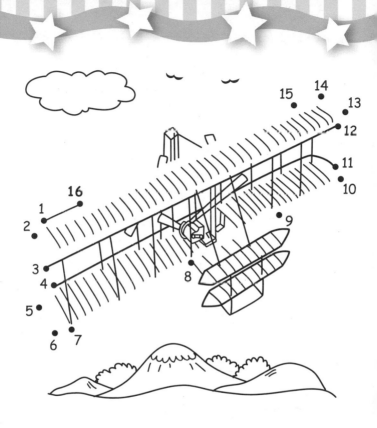

The Wright brothers, Orville and Wilbur, built and flew the first successful airplane in 1903. Connect the dots to see what it looked like.

START

END

George Washington, the first president, owned several horses. The one shown here was named Nelson. Show the president the path to take to reach Nelson.

Johnny Appleseed was a real person, John Chapman. He planted many trees across America. Put an X on the tree with the most apples, and draw a circle around the tree with the fewest.

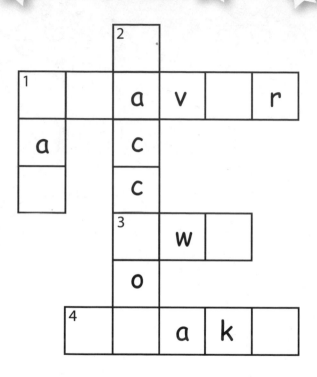

Many kinds of animals make their home in the Grand Canyon, a great American national park that's about as big as the state of Delaware.

1 down

1 across

3 across

2 down

4 across

Here are pictures of some of the animals that live in and around the Grand Canyon. Use the picture clues to solve the puzzle.

```
T P T W E N W A H
R A R A N G O H O
A N A G E R B O A
V P I O N E E R F
E I L N P W S S A
L T Y O X E N E K
```

WORD BOX

WAGON	TRAIL
TRAVEL	OXEN
PIONEER	HORSE

In the mid-1800s, pioneers heading west traveled the Oregon Trail in covered wagons. Use the word box to find and circle the words in the puzzle.

Ben Franklin invented eyeglasses so that he could see both near and far. Circle the two pictures of this famous American that are exactly the same.

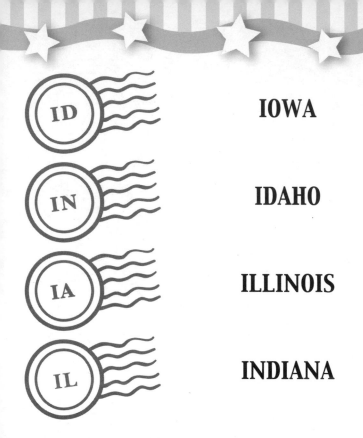

ID

IOWA

IN

IDAHO

IA

ILLINOIS

IL

INDIANA

Every state has an official two-letter postmark. The four on this page begin with "I." Draw a line from each postmark on the left to its state's full name on the right.

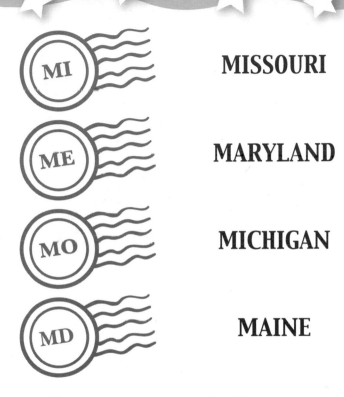

MI   **MISSOURI**

ME   **MARYLAND**

MO   **MICHIGAN**

MD   **MAINE**

Here are four more state postmarks, all beginning with the letter "M." Match each postmark on the left with its state's full name on the right.

On May 5, 1961, the astronaut Alan Shepard became
the first American to travel into space.

Now look closely at the picture of Alan Shepard. Five things have changed! Find and circle them all.

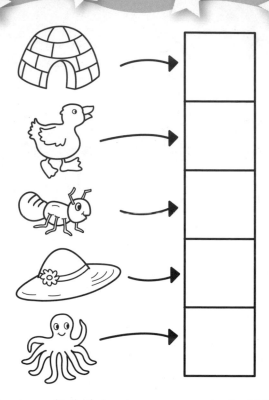

About one-third of the potatoes grown in the U.S. are from farms in this state. Write the first letter of each picture in the box to spell the state's name.

In Baltimore, Maryland, on June 24, 1784, thirteen-year-old Edward Warren became the first American to ride in a hot-air balloon. Have fun decorating the balloon!

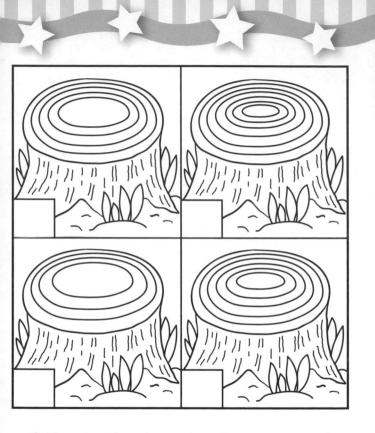

California's redwoods are the tallest trees on earth. They live for thousands of years! Count the rings on these tree trunks to find their age. Write the numbers in the boxes.

START

END

The longest river system in the U.S. is the Mississippi-Missouri-Ohio. Help the riverboat in the picture find its way home by showing it the right path.

Vermont is the largest producer of maple syrup in the United States. Design a label for this bottle of maple syrup.

① HUAT

③ CROOOLAD

② RIZNOAA

④ WEN XMECIO

1._____ 3._____

2._____ 4._____

The Four Corners is the only place in the United States where four states meet together. Unscramble the words and write the names of the states in the blanks.

Millions of bison roamed the American West during the 1800s. Circle the two bison that are exactly alike.

Prairie dogs live in burrows in states such as Texas, New Mexico, and Montana in the desert and plains areas. Connect the dots to see what a prairie dog looks like.

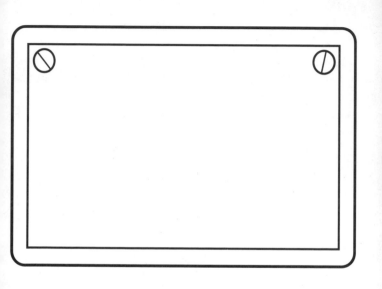

The first license plate for an American car was issued in Denver, Colorado, in 1908. Design your own license plate using the blank one on this page.

The Cardinal is the official bird of the states of Illinois, Indiana, Kentucky, North Carolina, Virginia, and West Virginia. Color the picture of this popular bird using the code.

B = ☆   T = 🌙   G = ☀   I = ✿

H = ☁   U = 🍎   L = 🍃

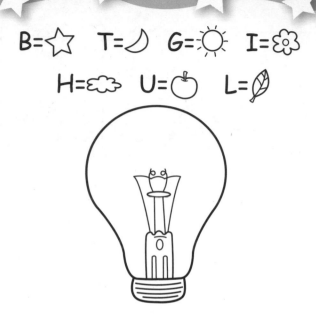

___ ___ ___ ___ ___ ___ ___ ___ ___
🍃 ✿ ☀ ☁ 🌙 ☆ 🍎 🍃 ☆

Thomas Alva Edison was one of the greatest American inventors. Use the code at the top to find out what Edison invented in 1879.

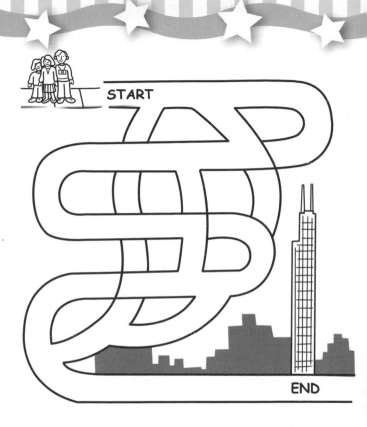

START

END

Standing at 1,450 feet, the Sears Tower, in Chicago, Illinois, is the tallest building in the United States. Help the people find their way to this popular tourist attraction.

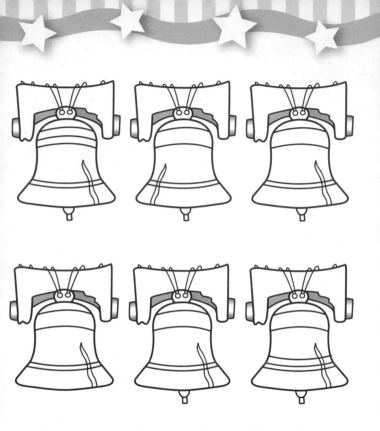

The 2,000-pound Liberty Bell came from England to Philadelphia in 1752. It cracked the first time it was rung. Find and circle the two Liberty Bells that are exactly alike.

F	S	E	G	T	M	M	V
U	T	H	O	D	F	T	E
D	M	A	S	U	G	E	M
V	G	L	W	A	I	I	D
G	U	T	S	E	O	O	S
D	E	S	O	U	F	L	M
F	L	L	U	V	E	F	V

Cross out the letters that appear four or more times. The letters that are left spell out in order the name of the fiftieth state. It joined the Union on August 21, 1959.

39

Abraham Lincoln was the sixteenth American president. Circle the picture of Lincoln as he appears on a five-dollar bill. He should have a beard and a bowtie, but no eyeglasses and no smile.

This American author published his "modern" English language dictionary in 1828. His first name was Noah. Color in *only* the books with uppercase letters to find out his last name. Then write it in the blanks.

41

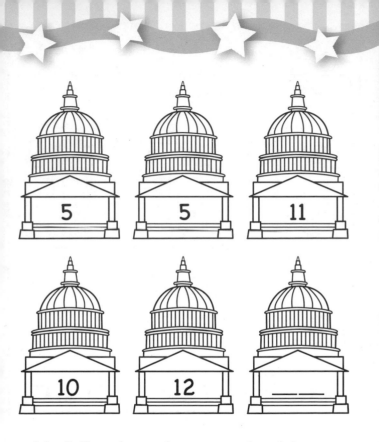

John F. Kennedy was the youngest elected American president. Add the numbers on the Capitol building. Then write President Kennedy's age when elected in the blanks.

42

Wyoming is the home of Yellowstone, the first American national park. Old Faithful Geyser is the most popular sight. Help this tourist find his way to Old Faithful.

Sculptors carved likenesses of the heads of George Washington, Thomas Jefferson, Theodore Roosevelt, and Abraham Lincoln into Mount Rushmore, in South Dakota.

44

The picture of Mount Rushmore has changed! Find and circle five things that are different from the picture on the opposite page.

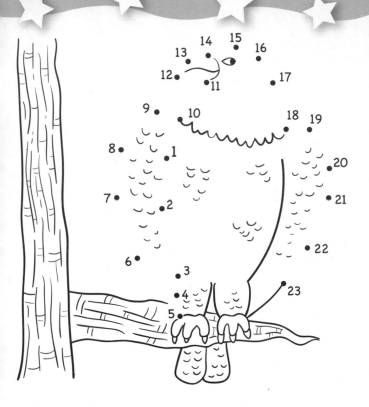

The Bald Eagle is America's national bird. Its wingspan can reach seven feet across! Connect the dots to see a picture of this majestic animal.

46

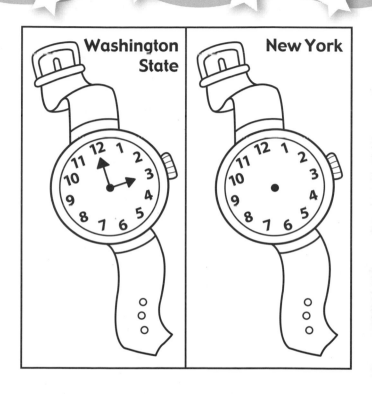

In 1870, the United States began to use time zones. So, when it is 3:00 in Washington State, it is 3 hours later in New York. Fill in the correct time in the New York watch.

FLEW ACROSS THE

__TL__NT__C

__C____N

Amelia Earhart was the first American woman to do this alone. Write the vowels A, E, I, or O in the blanks to spell out the answer.

CODE

⟨A⟩=N ☼=V ☁=T ☾=K

✕=F ∑=S △=E ◇=R

♡=A ☆=O ◎=L I=I

Who was the only President to serve for more than 2 terms?

$$\overline{✕}\ \overline{◇}\ \overline{♡}\ \overline{A}\ \overline{☾}\ \overline{◎}\ \overline{I}\ \overline{A}$$

$$\overline{◇}\ \overline{☆}\ \overline{☆}\ \overline{∑}\ \overline{△}\ \overline{☼}\ \overline{△}\ \overline{◎}\ \overline{☁}$$

Use the shape code at the top of the page to solve this riddle. Write the answer in the blanks.

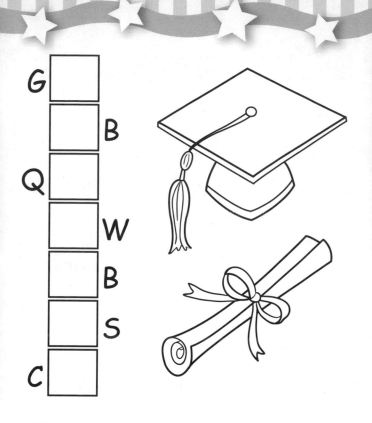

The oldest university in America was founded in 1636. To find out its name, fill in the boxes with the letter that comes before or after each letter given.

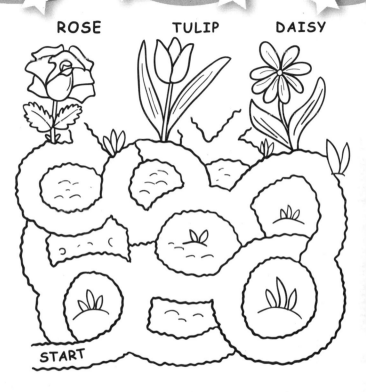

ROSE   TULIP   DAISY

START

The official flower of the United States was chosen in 1986. Only one path in the maze will lead to this flower. Find out what it is by following the right path.

Solutions

I = ✐ L = ✿ F = ○ O = ✳
R = ✖ C = □ A = ⚘ N = ✱

C A L I F O R N I A
□ ⚘ ✿ ✐ ○ ✳ ✖ ✱ ✐ ⚘

page 5

HET = T H E
EITWH = W H I T E
OSHUE = H O U S E

page 6

M
O
O
N

page 7

page 9

54

page 10

AMERICAN

CAR	NEAR
RAN	NAME
ARE	NICE
CAME	RAIN
CAN	MAIN
MAN	MEAN
EAR	RACE
CARE	CANE

(possible answers)

page 11

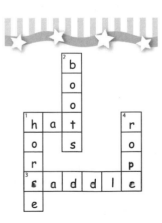

page 12

▲ = N ● = G ◇ = B ◎ = L

☽ = I ◨ = C ♔ = A ☆ = O

page 14

55

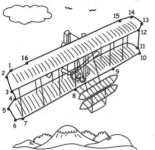

page 15

page 16

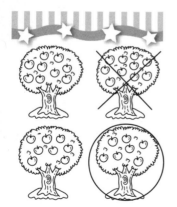

page 17

page 18

		r				
b	e	a	v	e	r	
a		c				
t		c				
		o	w	l		
		o				
s	n	a	k	e		

56

page 20

page 21

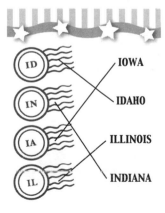

page 22

MI — MISSOURI
ME — MARYLAND
MO — MICHIGAN
MD — MAINE

page 23

page 25

page 26

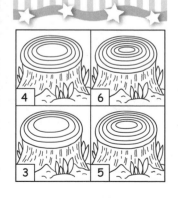

page 28

page 29

1. HUAT
2. RIZNOAA
3. CROOOLAD
4. WEN XMECIO

1. <u>UTAH</u>   3. <u>COLORADO</u>
2. <u>ARIZONA</u> 4. <u>NEW MEXICO</u>

page 31

page 32

page 33

B=☆ T=🌙 G=☀ I=❄
H=🐚 U=🍄 L=🍃

L I G H T B U L B
🍃 ❄ ☀ 🐚 🌙 ☆ 🍄 🍃 ☆

page 36

59

page 37

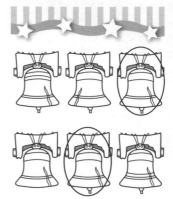

page 38

page 39

page 40

page 41

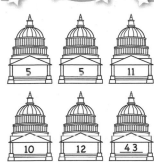

page 42

page 43

page 45

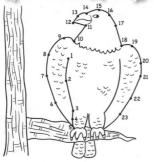

page 46

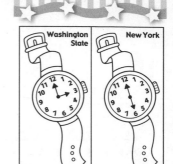

page 47

FLEW ACROSS THE

A TL A NT I C

O C E A N

page 48

CODE

🖐=N ☼=V 🦋=T 🌙=K

✖=F Σ=S △=E ◈=R

♡=A ☆=O ◎=L ▯=I

Who was the only President to serve for more than 2 terms?

F R A N K L I N
✖ ◈ ♡ 🖐 🌙 ◎ ▯ 🖐

R O O S E V E L T
◈ ☆ ☆ Σ △ ☼ △ ◎ 🦋

page 49

G | H
A | B
Q | R
  | V
  | A | W
  | R | B
  | R | S
C | D

page 50

ROSE   TULIP   DAISY

START

page 51